Please return / renew this item by the last date shown above
Dychwelwch / Adnewyddwch erbyn y dyddiad olaf y nodir yma

PONT *poetry*

First Impression—2002

ISBN 1 84323 088 7

© Phil Carradice

Phil Carradice has asserted his right under the
Copyright, Designs and Patents Act, 1988,
to be identified as Author of this Work.

This book is published with the support of the
Arts Council of Wales.

Printed in Wales at
Gomer Press, Llandysul, Ceredigion

Contents

Spooky Verses

Ghostly Riders

When night is dark
And wind is high
Then demons roam
And witches fly.

Over the moon
They're wandering free,
Their shadows stream
Like a wild dark sea.

Silent as death
Their black shapes bound,
Over the earth
Without a sound.

Silently gliding
Across the sky,
Those ghostly riders
Hurrying high.

The Cellar

There's a cellar in a mansion
Down a dark and leafy lane
And it rattles in the winter
In the whirling snow and rain.

The wind around the corners
Howls past like dying ghouls
But the cellar and its contents
Are waiting for you, fools!

Creep down the stairs and listen,
Push quickly through the door.
Nothing there, although you swear
Soft voices spoke before.

Stand rigid in the darkness,
The whispers will come back,
Around you in the blackness
The phantom voices pack.

Raw fear alive and breathing,
You know that evil's there.
You cannot see or touch it;
It lays your courage bare.

A shiver up your backbone –
They're crowding round your face!
Run screaming up the stairway
And leave this dreadful place.

Each time you pass that cellar,
Each time you see that stair,
Move quickly by. Remember –
That evil lurks down there.

The Vampire

In the sombre gloom of a silent room
The vampire waits, alone.
In a coffin deep he lies asleep,
His heart like solid stone.

But as the light fades into night
He rises from his tomb.
Into the street on silent feet
He glides with ghostly gloom.

In house and park, in doorway dark,
He searches for his prey.
A window wide? He slips inside.
He will taste blood today.

His fangs bite deep while victims sleep,
He drinks until he's done.
With bloodstained lips he homeward slips
Before the rise of sun.

And soon he lies with red-rimmed eyes
In Transylvanian soil.
His silent dreams are filled with schemes –
His blood begins to boil.

Throughout the day, while children play,
No fear of his attack,
His body's length regains its strength.
Come night time – he'll be back!

Hallowe'en

Hubble bubble, stir the pot
Before the good guys pinch the lot.
Throw in some salt and bits of string,
A black cat's eyes and dead bird's wing.
Let's brew a potion full of fear
Which looks and smells like home-made beer.
Add snails, a toad, a stagnant stream
And conjure up your last bad dream.

Now quick, before she calls a halt,
Drop teacher in – it's all her fault.
She said that we could use the oven
To magic up our witches' coven.
Three drops of custard from school lunch
Should finish off our potent punch.

Now drape yourself in witches' rags,
Under your eyes paint blue-black bags.
Let's dance from dusk till break of light
For no one sleeps on Hallowe'en night.

The Creature From Down In The Hall

I wonder who's hiding down under the stairs
Where it's black and it's damp and it's cold?
And why does he never appear in the day
When it's light and I'm feeling quite bold?

But when it grows dark and the wind starts to howl
I know that he's lurking down there,
I know that he's waiting to pounce out on me
As I go to my bed up the stairs.

So I hold on to Dad, I squeeze him so tight
And we rush like a train down the hall.
The creature can't catch us, whatever he does,
So I never get frightened at all.

But when I'm alone, tucked up in my bed,
The stairs start to creak and to call.
I know that he's prowling all over the house,
That creature from down in the hall.

Wizard and Witch Poems

I

Come magic spell, come demon witch,
Dump all our teachers in the ditch.

II

Hubble bubble, round we go.
Drink bird's nest soup and suck my toe.
Say the words, the magic pact –
Now all our teachers will get sacked.

III

Around the cauldron we shall go,
Three times high and three times low.
Add six bats, a parrot's wing,
Some broken toys and conker string.

Let's go to school just once a year
The rest is holiday – starting here.

IV

Eye of newt and toe of dog
Change our teacher to a frog.

In and Out
of the family

Who?

Who looks like a monkey
Caged up in the zoo?
You do.

Who makes me wash behind my ears
And stops me having fun?
You've got it.
My mum.

Who's that goodie-two-shoes
I would like to smother?
Correct.
My brother.

Who's got a face that's round and red
And ugly as a blister?
Who else?
My sister.

Who looks like a zombie,
Teeth yellow, breath so bad?
That's right.
My dad.

Whose father's sent him off to bed
Alone, without his tea?
Can you believe it?
Me!

How Do You Eat Spaghetti?

How do you eat spaghetti,
Those wriggly worms on your plate?
Tip them all in a jam jar
And use them for fishing, as bait.

How do you finish your homework
When friends keep on calling to play?
Say that you haven't got any
And do it some other day.

How do you get to watch telly
When Mum says it's time for your bed?
Pretend you're asleep on the settee
And watch it through one eye instead.

How do you dump the garbage –
Your games machine waits on its ledge?
Carry the trash down the garden
And throw it all over the hedge.

How do you tidy your bedroom
With clothes and your toys on the floor?
Gather them up in great armfuls
And drop them all into a drawer.

It's easy to make excuses
For things that you really don't like.
If everything fails, don't you worry –
Just turn round and go out on strike.

Cutting logs

Dad says put our jumpers on
and follow him outside.
The logs need cutting, so he says,
and we must help him
raise up large and painful
blisters on his hands.

And so we thunder through the door
and dive like black-backed
cormorants to grab
the handle of the axe.
But Dad puts out his hand
and gently takes the blade.

So we sit watching as he sweats
and grunts and splits the contoured wood
like matchsticks in the rain.
Later we go in and drink hot soup
and Mum says that she's glad
she's got three men around the house.

Burma Star

When I was little, knee high
to an ice-cream van,
I wore a cowboy suit
with blazing buck-skin fringes –
a regular Roy Rogers.

My father, smiling,
pinned his Burma Star
and his other bronze medallions
across my pigeon chest.
Like sheriff's stars I wore them.

I lost the medals, spinning,
falling in a graceful arc,
cut down by phantom gun-men
from a wild, imaginary west.

My father shrugged
and rubbed my hair
and for an instant, in his eyes,
I saw real soldiers coughing
blood-red death within the dark
and steaming jungles
of his past.

My Imaginary Friend

Tall as an oak tree
Standing in the yard.
Tough as a terrier,
Muscles big and hard.

Lumps across his forehead
Like he's been stung by bees.
Black hair long and greasy,
Full of jumping fleas.

Fingers fat as sausages,
His fist looks like a hammer.
He hits you and you feel as if
He hit you with a spanner.

Tiny eyes which glitter
Like a snake on the attack.
His teeth are all so rotten
He keeps them in a sack.

Ears like cauliflowers
Stuck up on his head.
Feet so big the local dogs
Can use them for a bed.

He really is so ugly
But you can still depend
Upon this gruesome creature
For he is my best friend.

Peter Pearce

Peter Pearce,
Very fierce.
Fists like lead,
"You – you're dead."
Ginger hair,
Doesn't care
Who he fights,
Day or night.
Steel-hard eyes,
Never cries.
Lives next door,
What a bore!
Standing there,
Out to scare
By his gate.
Feel the hate.
"Fight you now?"
"Don't know how."
Passing by,
Collar high,
Simple rule
Learned at school –
Don't annoy
This boy.

My Great Uncle

Uncle Eustace, very tall,
Doesn't need to stretch at all.
He found a job by luck and bribery
Dusting shelves in the local library.

When Granny Died

When Granny died they lined the streets
And rain came down in solid sheets.
I stood beside her coffin – crying.

Big men in black, their boots so clean,
Such faces I had never seen,
Filed past the place where she was lying.

And as they frowned and shook my hand,
At five, I failed to understand
This solemn thing called death and dying.

When Granny died it's my belief
The adults wallowed in their grief
And missed a silent soul's sad flying.

History Jig-saw

Bitter Wind

I lived in caves and forests, out on the wind-swept hill.
The cold winds made me fierce and strong; they're
    pulling at me still.
Winds howled when I was hunting, they froze my
    blood-stained hands,
They roared when we were gathered in small and
    frightened bands.
Each evening as we sheltered, as we huddled round the
    fire,
The cruel winds blew bitter and blew the bright flames
    higher.
The winds were there when I was born and there the
    day I died;
They swept across our mountains and the plains so
    green and wide.
They're blowing still across my bones,
The empty graves, the cromlech stones –
For though my tribe is dead and gone
The bitter winds blow on and on.

Walls of Ancient War

Silence falls
On walls of greying stone.
Only birds and bats
Or scurrying brown rats
Now call it home.

Once there was life here.
Once soldiers lazed
Along the battlements,
Waiting for their lord
To call them off to war.

Bright tapestries on every wall
And fires burning in the hall.
Serving maids and men-at-arms
Danced lightly in the shadows,
Out there, beyond the torch light.
Nodding over hunted game
The lord and lady dozed.
Unknowing.

Now there are ruins,
The people gone, forgotten.
Except, on still and silent evenings
Some shadows do remain –
The scrape of a broken harp string
And the lisp of a bardic tale,
The legends of long lost heroes
In their search for a holy grail.

The castle keeps the memory
Of all it ever saw
In its towers and turrets of conflict
And its walls of ancient war.

The Roman Soldier

Along lonely ramparts a wild west wind blows
And hills lie before me in regular rows.
Like waves on the seashore they all roll away –
I stare at them glumly and wait for the day
When I can sail home, a veteran at last,
When long days of war and campaigning are past.

Up here in this fortress we wait and we know
That sooner or later the enemy'll show.
It's not for adventure we fight, far from home,
Or even the honour and glory of Rome.
It's because we are soldiers, there's no other way.
So we fight and they give us a fistful of pay.

When my duty is over the Bath House awaits,
Then a bottle of wine with my girl and my mates.
Some other poor sentry will watch through the night
The road through the hills – it runs out of sight.
The Emperor can scheme and can plan his next war
But I'll be asleep on the barrack-room floor.

For King and Parliament

The King's men came, they stole our corn,
Dressed in their silks and gold.
"To feed the army of King Charles",
Was all that we were told.
And they took young Tom and Harry
For soldiers to the crown,
As drummer boys they led the charge
But they were both cut down.

Next Cromwell's troopers, Ironsides,
Descended on our lands,
Each musketeer and pikeman
With blood upon his hands.
Then they put a Major General
In town to keep the law,
And he outlawed singing, dancing
And sent us off to war.

Though Parliament and King may fight
And soldiers keep patrol,
We couldn't care if Cromwell wins
Or King Charles gains control.
We only want to tend our crops,
To keep our families fed.
The Cavaliers and Roundheads?
I wish they all were dead.

Men Who Work Below the Ground

When coal and iron cursed our land
They turned the valleys black.
Men flooded here to make it rich
But very few went back.
The cholera and typhoid came
And took them off each year.
The only consolation was
A pitcher full of beer
For men who worked below the ground
And sweated blood to earn their pound.

Long hours and brutal lock-outs
Brought Chartists to the hills.
They tried to ease the workers' lot
And cure the valley's ills.
But there's nothing helps the widow
Or the orphan by the gate.
While owners reaped the profits
They sowed a crop of hate
From men who worked below the ground
And sweated blood to earn their pound.

The railway lines snaked southwards,
They took away the coal,
And with them went so many dreams,
Like water down a hole.
With broken limbs and battered lives
And dust on every lung –
"There has to be a better way",
A phrase so often sung
By men who worked below the ground
And sweated blood to earn their pound.

On Dowlais Top

On Dowlais Top I spend my day,
On Dowlais Top I earn my pay.
I work the iron, smelting ore,
It scars my hands and makes eyes raw.

While furnace flames light up the sky
Hills echo to the iron's cry.
And Crawshay rolls in wealth and style;
He builds his fortune, mile on mile.

But men like me live in the town
In dirty slums, one up, one down.
We live like dogs in these few rooms,
No running water, stinking fumes.

We came from Brecon to this place,
Each one with a smile upon his face.
We didn't know, we couldn't tell
That we were walking into Hell.

My children died before they grew.
Disease took one, the brickworks two.
My wife and I, we curse the day
That Merthyr took their lives away.

But Sundays when the heather blooms
We leave our filthy, haunted rooms
And walk the hills above the town
Where brambles, gorse and rocks look down.

For just one day we feel the breeze,
We stroll on grass and gaze at trees.
We wish once more we were at home
Where streams run clear and rabbits roam.

The dream soon dies when we go back
To dirty streets and furnace stacks.
For though we dream, my wife and I,
We're here in Merthyr 'till we die.

All the year round

The Rubbish Dump

Our rubbish dump
stands at the edge of town,
surrounded by a line of posts
like soldiers guarding secrets –
best dump I've ever found.

I love old rubbish –
cold, neglected, interesting.
I love
　　　brown cricket bats
　　　and broken chairs;
　　　old bits of tin
　　　from garden sheds;
　　　the skeleton frames
　　　of ancient bikes;
　　　and tyres to hang
　　　from trees, to swing on
　　　in the breeze.

Our rubbish dump
is like a foreign land,
exciting, different,
full of things to see.

It's got
　　　broken toys,
　　　discarded dolls,
　　　a sledge with
　　　only one
　　　remaining runner;

deserted cars
lined up around
the edge,
their windows
gaping open
like a dozen
empty mouths;
long lengths
of wire, bits of bed
and row on row
of prams
which lie across
the ground,
the waiting coffins
of the dead.

In our dump you can find
anything you want – until
your mum says that it's dirty,
must be taken back –
right now!
"What do you want with these?" she'll cry.
And for a moment
I am tempted to reply.

I could say
I build worlds
from bits of rubbish;
this car becomes
an aeroplane
to whisk me off

to distant lands;
these bits of wire
can be fashioned
into warrior spears
to fight off
warlike bands;
or maybe fishing rods
or useful tools
for keeping open
windows in the night.

I could say loads of things
and, one day, might.
Mostly I just smile.
Mothers never understand
the value of a pile
of rubbish.

Sometimes

Sometimes,
when I sit in the topmost
branch of the tallest tree
and gaze out,
kingly, regal in my pride,

It would be easy,
very easy,
to lift my arms
and float away
balloon-like,
innocent
and free,

To sail on
like a zeppelin
over cities, stately houses,
over mountains and the sea.

Then everyone would point
and old men shake their heads
and wise men wonder
asking, "How?"

But they don't
and I sit still and dreaming
in my tree.

Because I know
My mum would miss me
If I went.

Owl

Sad owl,
silent,
measuring
the day,
waiting
like a terror
for the night.

Kestrel

Kestrel – sad-eyed
Killer of the skies –
Hangs low and hovers
Over hedgerows.
Wings rapid
As a humming bird
Fall silent, close.
The kestrel dives.
His eye is fatal,
Victims catch it
And they die.

All The Year Round

A   for the angry wind in the night
U   for umbrella that's blown out of sight
T   for the turning of leaves on the trees
U   for the undergrowth, wet to my knees
M   for the magic of colours that glow
N   for the nights in our house, long and slow

W   stands for wet days of rain
I   for the icicles stuck to the drain
N   means my nose will turn runny and red
T   for the trees that are stark, bare and dead
E   for excitement – at last we have snow
R   for the robin, his breast all aglow

S   for the squirrels which dart down the ledge
P   for the primroses lining the hedge
R   for the rivers which ripple and run
I   for the insects which soon start to come
N   for new life, fat buds on the trees
G   for the garden with flowers and leaves

S   for the sun, so bright in the sky
U   says that under its rays we will lie
M   for those marvellous days by the sea
M   means there's muffins and jelly for tea
E   for the evenings that never grow dark
R   for the roundabouts, swings and the park

The Very Best Feeling In The World

The very best feeling in the world,
Better than toffee that's chewed and curled,
Is lying at night in your own warm bed
As the day unravels around your head,
When you think of the trees and the hills you climbed
And the games that you played and the rhymes you
  rhymed.
You know for sure as you drift off to sleep
That whether the snow lies six feet deep
Or whether the sun just shines all day
Tomorrow is there, to roam and play.

Maybe you'll go to the park or the beach
Or lie in that tree where the branches reach
Down to the coolness of water and stream.
Maybe you'll fish, throw stones or just dream.
But now, in your bed, your happiness soars
For tomorrow the world and its treasures are yours.

Meet the Author

I was born in Pembroke Dock – not in the dock itself, you understand, but in the town – more years ago than I care to remember.

As a young boy I was interested in two things: reading and rugby. And I suppose I devoted most of my time to them, so subjects like maths and science never had much of a chance. Many years later, nothing much has changed. I still hate maths and love sport. These days I watch rugby rather than playing it and golf has taken over a lot of my leisure time.

Reading? I'm usually reading two or three books at the same time, everything from history and biography to the latest Harry Potter adventure.

My first published stories were in the school magazine and I went on to write poems and stories when I started teaching myself. My first book came out in 1985 – a collection of stories about children in care, entitled *The Hour of the Wolf.* Since then I have written a further 19 books!

My first novel for children was *The Bosun's Secret*, a story which takes place in Cardiff over a hundred years ago, based on real people, real places and events. The same characters appear in the sequel, *The Pirates of Thorne Island.*

I hope you enjoy the poems. Sometimes my days are so packed that I don't have time to write. Then I tend to get up and write at three or four in the morning. See, a time and a place for everything.

[Note: Poems by Phil Carradice also appear in Pont anthologies such as *Look Out, Thoughts Like an Ocean* and *Second Thoughts*.]